Andrew & Ashley's EUROPEAN TOURS

KIDS TRAVEL GUIDE TO LONDON WITH ACTIVITY BOOK AND TRAVEL JOURNAL

THIS BOOK BELONGS TO

_____

No part of this book may be reproduced or transmitted in any form or by any means, electronic or mechanical, including photocopying, recording or by any information storage and retrieval system, without written permission from the publisher.

The information provided within this book is for general informational purposes only. While we try to keep the information up-to-date and correct, there are no representations or warranties, express or implied, about the completeness, accuracy, reliability, suitability or availability with respect to the information, products, services, or related graphics contained in this book for any purpose.

Their usage does not imply any affliation with or endorsement by the trademark holders or owners.

© Copyright 2023. Songe Publishing LLC, All Rights Reserved

KEEP TRACK OF WHAT YOU EXPERIENCE IN LONDON SO YOU CAN SHARE WITH FRIENDS AND FAMILY WHEN YOU RETURN.

Get the *London Travel Journal* here.

HERE'S WHAT WE'RE UP TO ON THIS TRIP!

Hi, my name is Ashley. My twin brother Andrew and I are really looking forward to sharing what we've learned and taking you on a tour of London's most popular attractions for kids like us. This town is rich in tourist sites with so much modern culture! So cool.

The great thing about traveling to the United Kingdom (UK) is that almost everyone speaks English – whether you can understand what they're saying or not is another thing. So it's easy to get around, ask questions, and read signs. You're going to learn words you've never heard – in English! But be on the lookout because the Brits drive on the other side of the road!

Most people will arrive on a flight to one of the many airports surrounding London, but the way you'll travel once here or when moving somewhere else in the country can get interesting. Pay close attention – you'll get the hang of it.

There are puzzles, activities, and even a trip planner to organize what you want to see with your family. If you're really on top of things, you'll skip the long lines too.

But first a little about where you're going and what we'll do:

- Discovering the islands of the United Kingdom — yep, London is on an island
- Things to know about the UK
- How we'll get around to discover all the cool stuff
- Test your knowledge with activities
- Now plan your trip!

Get your passports ready to be stamped, and welcome to London!

The Continent and Countries of Europe

Where in the World are the United Kingdom and London?

There are seven continents in the world, and Europe is one of them. Check out the map below to find the continent you live on.

ARCTIC OCEAN
NORTH AMERICA
EUROPE
ASIA
ATLANTIC OCEAN
PACIFIC OCEAN
AFRICA
PACIFIC OCEAN
SOUTH AMERICA
INDIAN OCEAN
AUSTRALIA
ANTARTICA

4

Europe is made up of four geographic areas. If we visited each of those areas, we'd see that the culture-things like food, art, music, and interests, can sometimes be similar within each of the regions. Join me on this tour to find out more!

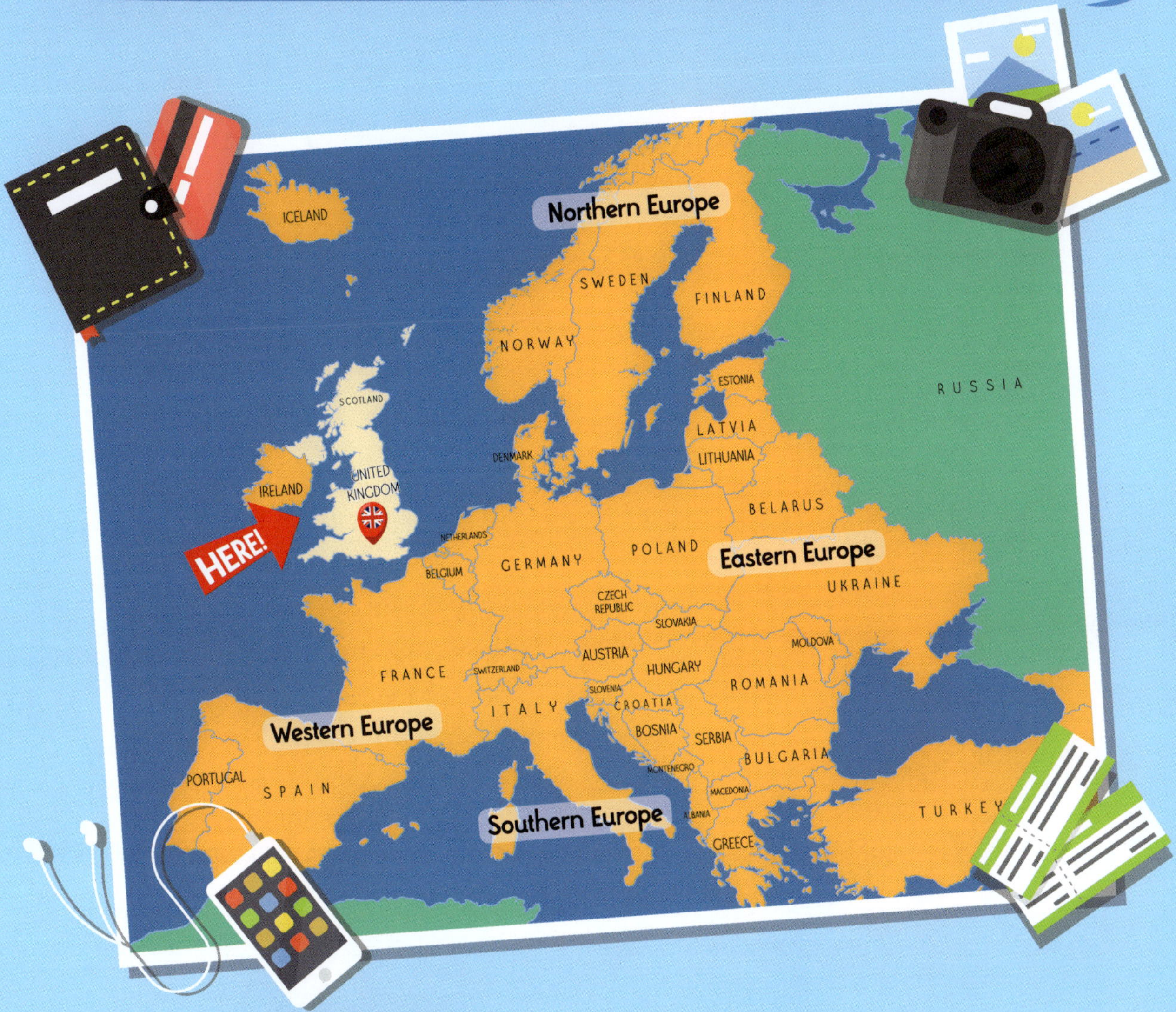

DID YOU KNOW? There are 51 countries that make up Europe.

About the United Kingdom

There is so much more to discover in the United Kingdom, but we're going to focus on just the cool stuff in London — the UK's capital city!

First of all, the United Kingdom is a set of islands. So the way to get into the country is to fly on an airplane OR arrive by ferry OR enter via the English Channel in an underground train. Yes, you get in your car and park on the train, and in 35 minutes or so you have crossed the English Channel! Cool, right?

The United Kingdom, also referred to as the UK, formed its current union in 1922 and is made up of four countries: England, Scotland, Northern Ireland, and Wales. You're traveling to London which is in England — within the United Kingdom. These countries govern themselves but are supported by the UK.

The UK also has dominion relationships with Canada, Australia, New Zealand, Newfoundland, and South Africa, but I'll leave it to you to learn that on your trip. That's too much to cover in this book!

What to Know About the UK & London

- The United Kingdom is made up of many islands, with 4 countries.

- The population of the United Kingdom is roughly 67 million people.

- The population of England is 56 million people.

- The population of the greater London area is almost 9 million people.

- Some parts of London have been inhabited since as early as 4000 BC!

- The capital of Great Britain is London.

- Great Britain is about 94,000 square miles - a bit larger than say the state of Oregon in the US, which is almost 95,000 square miles.

- In the UK, the distance from Land's End to John O'Groats is 837 miles long and would take you 14-16 hours to drive without breaks! To compare, it would take you about 12 hours to drive from the top of California to the southern border of Mexico.

- Also, Oregon has 4.4 million residents compared to the UK which has 67 million residents. That's a LOT of people living on those islands compared to that one US state!

- Official language: English!

- Over 300 languages are spoken in London - it's a very diverse population.

- The world's oldest tube (subway) network of underground trains is in London!

Each of the four countries within the UK has its own flag. See if you can spot them during your travels.

England

Scotland

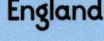

Northern Ireland

Wales

The UK's currency is the **British Pound**. The British Pound symbol is £ And the coins are called pence.

Bank notes (paper) come in £5, £10, £20, £50 and £100. Coins are called pennies or "pence" (abbreviated and spoken of as "p") and come in 1p, 2p, 5p, 10p, 20p, 50p amounts. It's funny that most people don't say "pence" they'll say "p." Coins also come in £1 pound and £2 pound versions. The former Queen of England had her image on most of the currency, but since her death after the crowning of her son Charles as king, it will be his mug (face) that appears on the currency — at some point in mid-2024.

9

What to Know About the UK & London

We are about to explore one of the most culturally rich destinations in the world. The UK's culture — which is the ideas, customs, and social behavior of a particular people or society — is really fun. There is so much to cover, and we can't tell you about everything, but that will be your adventure when you get there. Visit as many museums, monuments, restaurants or theaters and go on as many tours as you can! Learn for yourself what you love, like, or can leave.

Brits drive on the left side of the road, and the driver's seat is on the right side of the car!

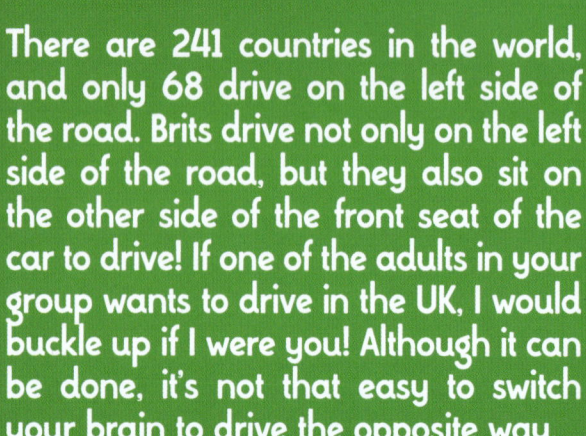

DID YOU KNOW?

There are 241 countries in the world, and only 68 drive on the left side of the road. Brits drive not only on the left side of the road, but they also sit on the other side of the front seat of the car to drive! If one of the adults in your group wants to drive in the UK, I would buckle up if I were you! Although it can be done, it's not that easy to switch your brain to drive the opposite way.

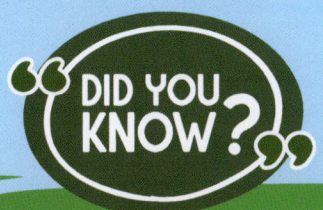

DID YOU KNOW?

There is a **"Right to Roam"** law in England that says you can walk across private property if it is in the mountains, moors (uplands), or heaths (infertile soil — weeds probably) and downs. So if you want to walk, run, watch wildlife and climb, you're golden. Farmers frequently create a path for hikers across their land which is divided by fences with gates so the cows and horses can't get across but the people can. If you really wanted to, you could walk from the top of Scotland to the bottom of England. Try doing that in other parts of the world without getting blocked by private property signs.

How Will I Get Around When I Get There?

Your flight to the UK may be a very long one depending on where you're coming from. It may be overnight — so pack your pajamas and this book to keep you busy! Don't forget your passport!

Once you get to the UK, you'll find that public transportation is a well-organized but complex labyrinth of trains, underground trains, double-decker buses, and black taxis. And, **the famous London Double Decker Bus** serves as the Hop-on, Hop-off bus tour — which now includes a water taxi. The tour is really good! After all, 67 million people need to get around an island which is about the size of Oregon in the US! London's underground system is called **The Tube.**

 **TRAVEL TIPS**

Plan ahead to buy tickets during busy times and consider getting an **Oyster card** so you don't have to stop to buy tickets every time you use public transport. This card allows you to add credit to it, so you can ride The Tube until the money runs out. Then you can "top it off" at any kiosk (that means add more money). Most kiosks have attendants and everything you need to know is online. Study the train map before you head out. The travel routes are color-coded, so it may take some thinking to plan your journey. You can always search on the internet in a GPS app for your destination, then press the little cable car icon and it will tell you which trains, buses, or underground to take.

12

DID YOU KNOW?

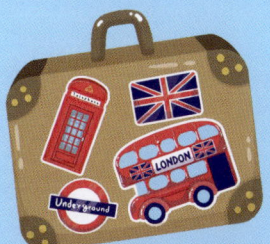

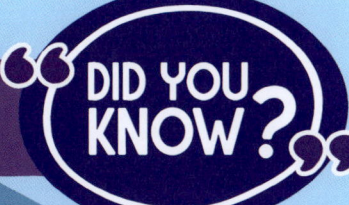

There is a tunnel for trains that crosses the English Channel – under the water!

A passenger train called **Eurostar** passes under the **English Channel** to get to other European countries, and of course if you want to drive, you can take the **le shuttle** train through the **Eurotunnel.** How cool is that!? It takes about 30 minutes to cross over to Callais, France from Folkstone, UK. The other option is to take a ferry across the channel but it takes a lot longer and you might get seasick.

eurostar

EURO TUNNEL

DID YOU KNOW?

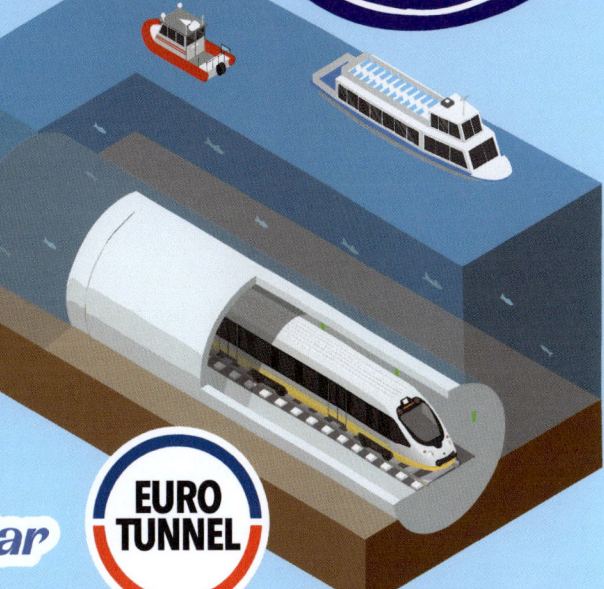

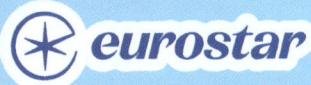

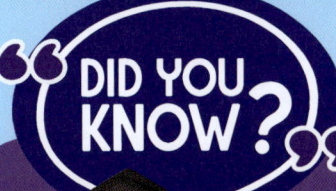

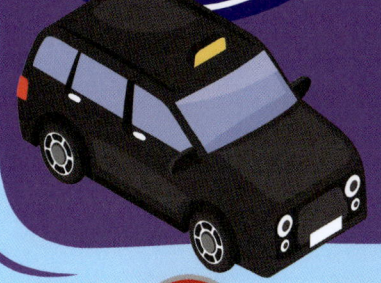

The black taxis in London are very famous. They're called the **Hackney Carriage or Black Cab.** The drivers have to train for almost a year to memorize every street, famous landmark, and facts about their beloved city. That's a lot to know! App taxis are also available in London, but they won't know as much about the city. Ask your driver about something you learn in this book!

TRAVEL TIPS

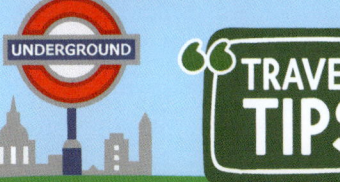

Be on the lookout for the **Underground** sign which is your cue to get on **The Tube!** Streets are pretty busy with shops so it may not be obvious. Do your research ahead of time to load the best app on your phone to be in-the-know and buy tickets on-the-go.

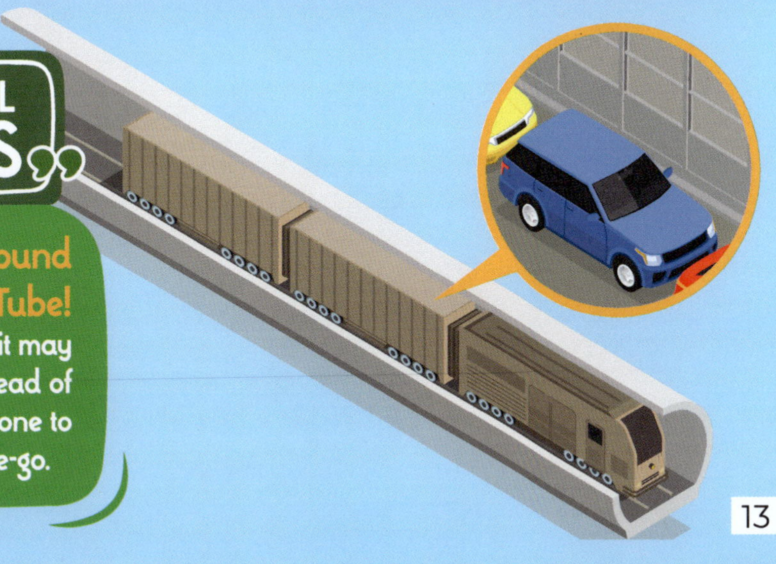

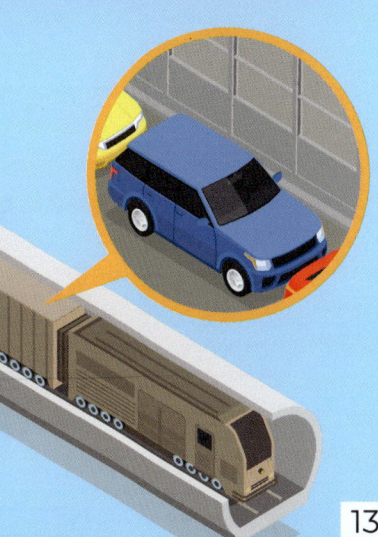

Discovering the UK & London

You're going to see a lot of exciting things in London. One of them is where the UK's central government operates and another is where the Royal Family works and lives. Yes, the UK has a King and Queen! Did you know that?

The United Kingdom has a **Parliament** much like the US House of Representatives (the lower house of Congress) in Washington DC. It's where most high-level legislative decisions are made for the people of the UK. Except in this country, there is a **prime minister, lords and ladies,** and **MPs**: which stands for "Members of Parliament." That's a much longer story that you can learn more about when you visit. But you've got the basics. Be on the lookout for lords and ladies who wear wigs! Wait, WHAT? (But only on special occasions!)

The House of Parliament is in a very famous London building called Westminster. It's built on the River Thames (prounounced "tems") with a big clock tower called Big Ben! In the tour section, you'll learn more about that!

London is represented to the world by a monarchy — that means a royal family — who do loads of things like show up at charity events! Do you know who the King of England is? His name is Charles and he and his wife live in London at Buckingham Palace. More on that later!

There are some famous schools and universities in the UK that you've probably heard about in the movies.

- Eton
- University of Oxford
- University of Cambridge
- University of St. Andrews

- London School of Economics and Political Science
- Imperial College

- Hogwarts (No, just kidding! Only in the books and movies!)

Harry Potter's Hogwarts School of Witchcraft and Wizardry looks like some of these schools, but this one only exists in books and in the movies! Don't miss the Warner Brothers Studio Harry Potter tour which we'll talk about later!

15

A Little UK History

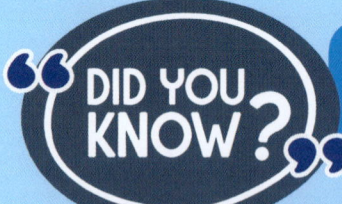

DID YOU KNOW?

There are over 4,000 **stately homes** (very large houses) in the UK. Some are restored to their original glory and some are ruins. They were built a long time ago.

CULTURE ALERT

Ever heard of the **TV show Downton Abbey?** Yep, TV shows and films are included in a country's culture. And the UK pumps out, among other things, a lot of "period films" and TV series. Most likely one of the adults in your family have watched Downton. It was filmed at a stately home called **Hampshire's Highclere Castle** which is 2 hours southwest of London. You can tour that site as well, but there may not be enough time to take a driving trip like that. The aristocratic Crawley family in the TV series lived there during the period from 1912-1926.

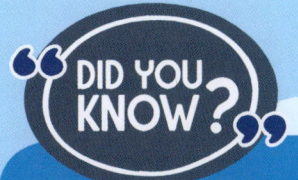
DID YOU KNOW?

Why were castles built in the first place? At some time between the year 1000 and 1600, castles with walls were built to protect citizens from invaders. They usually included a great tower to serve as a lookout with the fortified wall to keep invaders out.

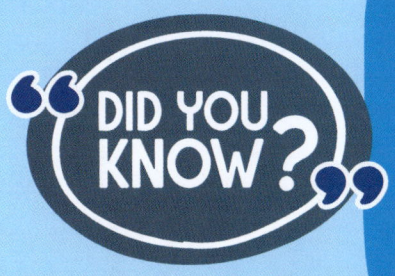
DID YOU KNOW?

In the late 1500s, fortified (thick and high) walls were no longer needed so the sophisticated and wealthy built and lived in stately homes (very large houses) as a show of wealth. Many gained their family wealth from making and exporting products. England's past generations sailed around the world during this time to find new markets in other lands where they could buy and sell goods. It was a time of extreme prosperity.

17

A few famous UK & London Culture Fun Facts!

There is so much culture to share as London and the UK are famous in many categories. We'll just show you our favorites for kids and stuff you should be in the know about! We can't include them all. So before your trip to London, do your research!

"CULTURE ALERT"

The next few pages include one big culture alert. You won't believe how Brits express themselves in so many ways. It's never dull in London!

London and UK are known for:

Music
- The Beatles
- Rolling Stones
- Ed Sheeran
- Adele
- Harry Styles
- Coldplay
- Spice Girls

This is a print of a famous photo of the Beatles crossing Abbey Road. You can visit the crossing, walk it yourself and make the same pose in a photo. Lots of people do! The Fab Four (the group's nickname) recorded most of their music in a studio there between 1962 and 1970. Ever heard of them? Ask an adult or go online to find out!

Theatre

If you like a good play or musical, you can find some of the best productions in London. Try to take in one of them if you have time.

- Peter Pan
- Oliver
- Mama Mia!
- Cats
- Dr. Dolittle
- Shakespeare

Artists

There are many famous artists. Make time to visit London's museums to learn about them.

- Henry Hudson
- David Spriggs
- John Constable
- Philip Colbert
- Henry Moore
- Banksy is one of them!

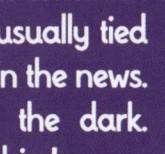

Banksy is a mysterious artist who chooses walls in the UK on which to paint statements — usually tied to something going on in the news. He does his work in the dark. Nobody has ever seen him!

Authors, Books, & Movies

There are many famous ones you'll recognize! The one's mentioned here need no introduction. Which ones do you know? Have you read these books or seen their movie versions?

- Paddington Bear
- James Bond
- Sherlock Holmes
- Mary Poppins
- Harry Potter
- Shrek

The Royal Family

England's Royal Family is world-famous. King Charles' coronation was live on TV not long ago when he and his wife were officially crowned King and Queen of England. This royal life doesn't come without **paparazzi** following them around and the family being in the news for any or no reason at all. Did you know that Prince Harry married an American actress and has moved to Los Angeles?

Prince William and Kate, his wife, have three children. William is the next in line to the British throne, so all eyes are on him and his family. You'll see pictures of all of them in the newsstands around London.

Make sure to do the Buckingham Palace and Mews tours to learn more about all of this!

Fashion

London design and fashion houses have always had a big influence on what the world wears. Even "posh" kids get into it! Have you ever heard the word "posh" before? It means upper class or expensive!

Famous fashion designers and brands from London include:

STELLA McCARTNEY (yes, her Dad is one of the Beatles mentioned earlier)

VICTORIA BECKHAM (married to the famous footballer (soccer player) David Beckham)

BURBERRY  **ALEXANDER McQUEEN**

BURBERRY ESTABLISHED 1856

Horseback Riding, Racing, & Equestrian Competitions

There are many horse racing events and competitions in England. Some are very "posh" (fancy) — like the Royal Ascot — and English society and royalty turn out dressed in their best formal clothes. Sometimes the men wear "tops and tails" (a top hat and tuxedo tails) and the women a fancy dress and a "fascinator" hat! What would a Brit say? "It's all very civilized!"

Media

London's newspapers, whether online or in print, are well known for gossip and making a big deal out of nothing! The royal family and celebrities are followed by the paparazzi (news photographers) constantly — so it is difficult for them to have private lives. Photo captions sometimes make up stories that may not be true. Can you imagine! Check the newsstands when you're there.

Here are some good conversation starters that certain Brits like to talk about. There's something for everyone.

The countryside is lush outside and inside of London, and Brits are very proud of their gardens. Every year they have an event called the **Chelsea Flower Show** where garden designers compete for prizes. It is a very coveted award. Ask the right person about their garden — they will likely have a lot to say.

Gardening

Antiques

The famous UK **Antiques Roadshow** TV show is also aired in the US. The hosts talk to locals in different locations (usually filmed in the garden of a stately home — a very grand house indeed!).

Museums & Auctions

Some of the best museums in the world are to be found here. They house very famous, important paintings, sculptures and historical artifacts like dinosaur skeletons! Don't miss out! London hosts very posh auctions of fine art — and these pieces can go for multi-millions of pounds or dollars! A masterpiece by Gustav Klimpt sold for 85.3 million pounds making it the most expensive piece of art ever auctioned in Europe.

English, You Say?

Is that English or English, sir?

One of our favorite things about London is the way that English people have different words for things — or they say something differently — but they are speaking English! There are words like tomato — where they would say "tow-maa-tow." Yep, it's true. And you're going to ask yourself at some point: "Are we speaking English?"

BRITISH WORD	AMERICAN TRANSLATION	BRITISH WORD	AMERICAN TRANSLATION
Let's have a brew	Let's have a cup of tea	Rubbish	Garbage
Let's have a cuppa	Let's have a cup of tea	Holiday	Vacation
Bits	Your things or stuff	Pavement	Sidewalk
Mate	Friend	Petrol	Gas
Jolly good	Very good	Shopping trolley	Shopping cart
Chips	French fries	Starter	Appetizer
Crisps	Potato chips	Chap	Man, guy
Biscuit	Cookie	Bob's your uncle	There you have it or it's done.
What's for tea?	What's for dinner?	Mashup	Recorded music that has parts of different songs or images
Y'alright?	How are you?		
Sorted	All set, fixed, done	Telly	Television or TV
Copper	Policeman	Abbey	Church
Posh	Fancy or expensive	Cheerio	Hello and goodbye!
Suss	Figure out, guess	Jolly good!	Very good!
Football	Soccer	Blimey!	OMG
Quite	A little bit		

DID YOU KNOW?

Do you know what an accent is? The Brits speak English but they say certain words differently, which they learned to pronounce in their region of the UK.

The phrase "Bob's your uncle" is slightly old-fashioned, but you may hear adults say it. It comes from 1887 when the English prime minister named Robert (Bob for short) Gascoyne-Cecil appointed his nephew Arthur Balfour as Chief Secretary. He was able to get things done because — you guessed it — Bob was his uncle!

23

What you'll see, hear, smell, and taste...

You're going to see, hear, smell, and taste a lot of new things, but you'll also be able to find some familiar things too. Don't worry, you will be able to speak English to ask questions and all the signs are in English. You might need to have a little patience when SUSSing things out. You'll also find some good things to eat in London! One of our favorites is **Fish & Chips! (Chips = fries.)** Not to worry if fish is not your thing, there are lots of choices like pizza and Indian curries which are some of the best in the world!

Here's some stuff you should try! I love the fish and chips and Ashley can't get enough of the scones with clotted cream and jam.

- Fish & Chips - battered and deep-fried fish filets and fries
- Scones with clotted cream & jam - a yummy biscuit with cream and jam
- Shepherd's Pie - a baked dish with ground meat and potatoes
- English Breakfast - eggs, bacon, sausage, stewed tomatoes and toast
- Bangers and Mash - sausages and mashed potatoes
- Sunday roast - roasted meat, roast potato, Yorkshire pudding (like a biscuit or roll) and peas!
- Toad in the Hole - sausage with gravy and vegetables
- Cornish Pasty - meat baked inside a pastry shell
- Steak and Kidney Pie (I'll stick to the Fish & Chips, thank you!)

Famous Products you can try that are sold in other countries too!
- Cadbury chocolate
- Walkers crisps (potato chips)
- Walkers shortbread biscuits (cookies)
- McVities's biscuits (cookies)
- Cathedral City cheese (Cheddar - yum!)

It's safe to say you'll likely eat lunch or dinner in a pub at some point. At last count, there are roughly **3500 pubs** in London. You can't go very far without spotting one! It's where people in the neighborhood go to meet. Keep your eyes peeled in London. You'll be able to find familiar food and restaurants from the US and other countries that you recognize. As we said, this is an international city! Which ones did you find? *Keep track of them in your travel journal when you get there. But kids can't go pubs without an adult! Just saying.*

25

London Sports

London is well known as a world competitor in many sports!

LONDON AREA PROFESSIONAL SPORTS

There are 20 professional sports stadiums in the London area alone. That's a lot! So you could say sports are a big deal here.

- Football (you may know it as soccer) - 5 teams in the London area
- Rugby - Kinda like football
- Cricket - They break for tea!
- Tennis - Wimbledon Tennis Tournament (very posh!)

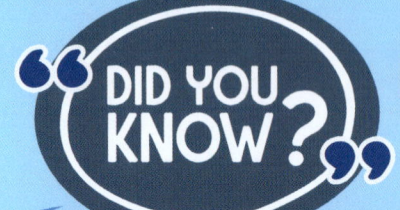      

David Beckham is a world-famous former football (soccer) star player from the UK who became famous while at Manchester United. He is also an underwear model! BLIMEY! Back to football. David is known for his range of passing, crossing ability and bending free-kicks as a right winger. Today he is co-owner of both the Inter Miami and Salford City football teams. And, oh yeah, also married to Victoria Beckham — the famous former Spice Girl and now a fashion designer. They are a famous London celebrity couple.

THE OLYMPICS

The Brits take their sport quite seriously — as they should. They are a major contender in the world Olympic Games. The Summer Olympics have been hosted in London three times: in 2012, 1908, and 1948. London Stadium is where the Olympics were hosted in 2012.

There are many more casual sports events enjoyed by the locals too.
- Polo
- Rowing or Sculling
- Formula 1
- Horse Racing

CULTURE ALERT

The fans can be quite enthusiastic at football matches (games). They are well known for supporting their team, wearing jerseys, waving flags, and yelling inside the stadium. It can get really loud! I would recommend public transportation if you go to a match. There can be a lot of traffic before a game.

Welcome to London!

Hi, it's **Andrew**. Ashley's twin brother. Welcome to London! There is so much to see and do, so we'll only feature our favorite things on this trip. One of my favorites is that London is a very international city. So you'll also see and meet people who live here that are originally from many different countries. One word of caution though: be careful when crossing the street in London as they drive on the other side of the road! You'll want to look for traffic coming from the left, but they come from the right as you step off the curb. Other than that, you are going to see, hear, smell, taste, and experience a lot of new things. But don't worry, we've done it before and, trust me, you're going to like it!

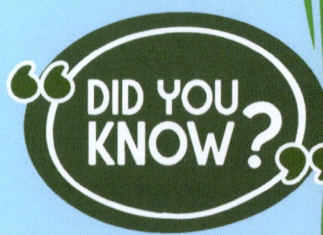

The Brits drink a LOT of tea — 100 million cups a day in fact. When there is a major event on the telly (TV), people like to brew a "cuppa" (a cup of tea) just before the event. It's called **The Great British Kettle Surge!** The energy department has to be on special alert to manage the surge of power needed to heat up all those tea kettles!

Here's a short list of some things you'll want to know upfront:

Official language: English

What the British call themselves: Brits

What you call a friend or acquaintance: Mate

Most likely place to have lunch: A pub!

Famous drink: Tea!

Our favorite things to eat: Fish & Chips, Shepherd's Pie, Scones with Clotted Cream, Curry, and Cornish Pasties

What to wear: It rains a lot in London. Be sure to pack a lightweight rain jacket with a hood and a sweatshirt! Even if it's summer. Otherwise, dress casually.

My favorite British English words: Jumper (sweater), boot (trunk), chips (french fries), crisps (potato chips), dustbin (garbage can/waste-paper basket/bin), lift (elevator)! More on page 23.

London is known for films & fashion: Be on the lookout for models and actors!

Famous products: Delicate porcelain tea sets like Royal Worcestor and Wedgwood, and cars like Aston Martin, Bently, Jaguar, and Land Rover.

Look and listen to the world around you. Ashley likes the Harry Potter tour — she's read every book and has seen every movie too. And she also likes the tour of the Royal Mews. And I'm a big sports fan, so I'm more likely to choose a professional football game. I also like the Maritime Museum. Do your research and find your favorites! Then plan your trip with your family on pages 48 through 50.

Here's Where We're Going on This Tour

We stayed in London for a week on our last trip. So, if you are visiting for a shorter period, take the best of this tour and pick your favorites.

London is split up into a few very unique districts. We'll start with one and move to the next. You may be traveling within these areas to get to restaurants or events — so make sure you pay attention to how to get around like we explained at the beginning of the book! Take the Tube — it's fast and fun. Or order a taxi to take in all the sites along the way. When you visit each place, you can learn more about everything it has to offer. The River Thames runs through London so sometimes it helps to get your bearings knowing where you are in relation to the river!

The Tube symbol looks like this. Look for it on the street to find out where the underground is.

" DID YOU KNOW ? "

30

Central London

WEST END
- Well-known theater district - Piccadilly Circus tube station
- Piccadilly Circus
- Piccadilly theater district

SOUTH BANK - WATERLOO TUBE STATION
- London Eye
- Shrek's Adventure
- London Dungeon
- London Aquarium

LONDON BRIDGE
- London Bridge
- Tower of London
- The Shard
- Borough Market
- HMS Belfast World War II ship
- Unicorn Theatre

GREENWICH
- Maritime Greenwich UNESCO
- National Maritime Museum
- Old Royal Naval College - Pirates!
- IFS Cable Car or Uber Boat to Greenwich

WESTMINSTER
- Buckingham Palace
  - Royal Mews - equestrian stables for the royal family (including the King's carriage made of gold!)
- The Palace of Westminster
  - Westminster Abbey
  - Big Ben tower tour
- 10 Downing Street
- London Eye

Let's Go!

London Trip Days 1 & 2

DAY 1

TRAVEL DAY, KEEP MOVING SO YOU DON'T GET JET LAG!

You just got to town after a long plane ride. So get settled in your hotel and choose something in the afternoon or evening to help you to stay awake. Maybe go to ride the London Eye, go for a walk in a city park, or take a boat ride on the Thames.

DAY 2

GET OUT TO SEE THE CITY!

It's going to be a busy day! Either set up your own transportation or take the hop-on-hop-off bus to get there. These two tours are incredible! Get on a Double-Decker bus full tour. Then get off at your favorite stops!
- **MORNING:** Buckingham Palace and Royal Mews
- **AFTERNOON:** Westminster

Where the king and queen live and work: **BUCKINGHAM PALACE**

And of course, there is also a palace! It's where the King and Queen of England reside, right in the heart of London. This famous building called Buckingham Palace. You might have seen this one on television during the royal wedding of Prince Harry and his American bride Meghan Markle! Did you hear about that? It was all over the tabloids (something like TMZ for you!)

You may not want to fill every morning and afternoon with tours, although it's nice to see as much as you can while you're there. Use the trip planner on page 48 to add a park visit, sporting event or perhaps **high tea** to your itinerary.

THE ROYAL MEWS

If you like horses, you're going to love this tour. It's where they handle travel arrangements for the King and members of the royal family. It's one of the finest working stables in existence today. You'll see everything from horses and carriages to cars and the livery or horse stables.

STOP #2

Where the government works: **WESTMINSTER & BIG BEN**

As we said earlier, **Westminster** is the place where big government decisions are made for the people and sometimes the rest of the world. London and the UK play a big role on the world stage. It might seem like a small country, but it's no lightweight when it comes to its influence on international affairs. Discover the building's history and heritage and find out about the work of the UK Parliament during a 90-minute guided tour. You can also book a tour of **Big Ben**. Fair warning though: **You have to climb 300+ steps!**

Trip Days 3 & 4

DAY 3  **LET'S HAVE A LITTLE FUN!**
MORNING & AFTERNOON:
- Warner Brother Studios
- Harry Potter Tour

Make sure to clear your schedule for the day of this tour. You're going to travel just outside London to get to **Warner Brothers Studios**. And if you're lucky, you'll get a reservation for a special event like a **"Family Dinner in the Great Hall"**. It's where Harry and his mates ate dinner together in the movies!

- Your options are either to take the bus transportation included in the tour or find your way there by taking the train to Watford.
- The train to Watford takes 20 minutes from London's Euston Station; the tour-provided bus ride from London takes a lot longer.

DAY 4

LONDON TOWER TOUR

Today is a mix of fun with some pretty amazing things to see. The **Tower of London** is an official Historic Royal Palace. It's London's history right before your very eyes! Remember we talked about the castles, manor houses, stately homes, and forts you might see? Well, this is one of them. It had the very important role of defending London as early as the year 1097. There are living quarters, knights with suits of armor, and even medieval torture chambers preserved the way they were back in the day. There were some pretty scary practices going on in the prison. Check it out on the tour!

34

MORNING: TOWER OF LONDON

TRAVEL TIPS

Be sure to reserve tickets for these tours well in advance. This is an award-winning tour, and it sells out early.

Changing of the Guard

Fort and Prison
- You've got to see it for yourself!

The Brits have a very famous ceremony to change the guard. At certain intervals during the day, they relieve the guards of their duties and replace them with others. In the process, the guards walk very stiffly and can't smile, no matter how much the crowd sometimes does to make them laugh! Set your watches so you don't miss it.

Crown Jewels

The Crown Jewels have been in the royal family for centuries. This exhibit contains some of the world's most valuable jewels, and it's clear that the British royals wanted to make their wealth known. When you see the jewels, you'll know what I mean! Today, when King Charles hosts a ceremony, sometimes he and his wife Queen Camilla wear their crowns displayed on this tour. Check it out! "It's extraordinary!" as the Brits might say.

DAY 4 CONTINUED

LUNCH: BOROUGH MARKET

TRAVEL TIPS

You can take an UBER Boat operated by Thames ("tems") Clippers to get from one destination to the next! How fun!

AFTERNOON: GLOBE THEATRE

Ever heard of the famous playwright and actor **Shakespeare?** Yes, you have! He was mentioned earlier in the book in our remarks on theater culture. The Globe Theatre was first opened in 1599 by the Lord Chamberlain's Men, the company that William Shakespeare wrote for and partly owned. The first play he wrote may have been Julius Caesar in 1599. You've heard of Romeo and Juliet? Shakespeare wrote that too.

Today's Globe Theatre is the third version of this national monument which has been rebuilt over time. It celebrates Shakespearean plays and takes you back to Shakespeare's London. Relive the iconic shows and get the chance to get ready for the stage yourself with interactive costumes and props. Yes, you get to try on costumes and wigs!

Trip Day 5 - 7

DAY 5 — THE NATURAL HISTORY MUSEUM & SHREK'S ADVENTURE

MORNING: NATURAL HISTORY MUSEUM

The Natural History Museum exhibits a vast range of specimens from various parts of our world's natural history. And, if you like learning and seeing dinosaurs, this is definitely the place for you! From prehistoric animals and plants to fossils to arctic exploration to bugs, fish, frogs: You name it.

And learn how modern science works to identify and study artifacts. You can see things up close and personal: Like the colossal titanosaur **Patagotitan mayorum** — one of the largest creatures to have ever walked our planet.

Suss out:
When did dinosaurs live?
What killed the dinosaurs?
What's the coolest dinosaur?
How are dinosaur fossils formed?

DID YOU KNOW?
The Isle of Wight in the UK recently discovered a treasure trove of fossils just off Britain's southern coast!

TRAVEL TIPS
Purchase tickets well ahead of your visit so you can avoid the lines, or worse, not get in at all!

DAY 5 CONTINUED

AFTERNOON: SHREK'S ADVENTURE

Shrek's Adventure is an interactive fairytale experience for kids and the kid's still inside many adults. Lots of fun to be had here. There's a flying magic double-decker bus, a swamp, a poison apple pub and DreamWorks® PlayStations. Visit their website and purchase your tickets ahead of time for sure.

TRAVEL TIPS

If you like these types of exhibitions, there are more in the same area. Sealife, The London Dungeons and the London Eye are also options. You can find combination tickets on the Shrek website.

DAY 6

WINDSOR CASTLE — The other Royal Family's Residence

Windsor Castle is a royal family residence with 1,000 years of history. It has been called home by over 40 monarchs (generations of royal families). It is fascinating to see how the royals live and entertain guests there. The castle is filled with treasures from the past, and there is a changing of the guard here too. The guards are there to protect the royals 24/7. If you've seen a royal wedding on TV, this is where it was likely held!

MORNING & AFTERNOON: WINDSOR CASTLE

TRAVEL TIPS

It's a one-hour train journey to and from the center of London but worth it. You can find a place for lunch or "tea" in the town of Windsor depending on the time slot you have tickets for. It will take you about 2 hours to properly visit the castle.

DAY 7

TRAVEL DAY TO YOUR NEXT DESTINATION

Typically on your last day in London, you'll be getting ready to travel home or to your next destination. If you have extra time, include something else fun in your plans – that could just be shopping! Otherwise cheerio and travel safe, mates! We spent the morning in Hyde Park. And, look who we met on the next page!

PLANNING YOUR TRIP

Your tour could look much different from this, depending on when you can get your tickets. Or perhaps you will decide you're not that interested in something. Make sure you plan carefully in the planning section of this book on pages 48 to 50.

TRAVEL TIPS

Remember to add airport transit time to your travel plans. If you're flying out of London, it takes time to pack, eat, and get to an airport in a big city. And you've got to be there at least 2 hours before the flight.

Who We Met in London on Our Last Trip!

"DID YOU KNOW?"

The **Corgi** is Ashley's favorite and a famous royal breed! It is formally called the **Pemberton Welsh Corgi**. It was former Queen Elizabeth's favorite dog breed. There were frequently photos of her walking her Corgis when she wasn't running the agenda of the Royal Family. Ever heard of Crufts dog shows on TV? Both the Corgi and the Jack Russell are official breeds.

We decided one sunny afternoon, during our trip, to visit **Hyde Park**. There, we saw other kids our age playing football! (or soccer to you — as you know now!). They asked us if we wanted to join in. Ashley and I both play soccer at home so we said yes! (After asking our parents of course.)

Welcome to London! Meet our dogs Merlin the Corgi and Poppy the Jack Russell Terrier!

The **Jack Russell** breed was named after Reverend John Russell, who bred one of England's finest strains of terriers for hunting. Most of the time Jacks are a beloved family pet, and on farms they keep the rats away. They're very clever. **Poppy** is a Parson Jack Russell which means she has longer legs than other types. She likes to chase miniature tennis balls!

Andrew & Ashley's EUROPEAN TOURS

TEST YOUR KNOWLEDGE WITH ACTIVITIES!

Now that you've learned a lot about London, let's test your memory and have a little fun. Remember, you can always go back to find the answers in the main part of the book.

TEST YOUR KNOWLEDGE OF THE TOUR!

DOWN

1. Name of the tallest building in London
2. The name of the tower clock at Westminster
3. The tour where you can experience everything Harry Potter
6. The name of the underground transport in London
8. The river that runs through London
9. Where does the Royal Family live and work in London?
12. Name the fort of London where the Crown Jewels are kept?

ACROSS

4. The royal family home in Windsor
5. The place where the royal horses and carriages are kept
7. Where does the Parliament work?
10. Which bus do you take for the Hop-On, Hop-Off tours in London?
11. The name of the body of water to cross from the UK to France
13. A museum that has life-sized dinosaurs
14. Theatre name where Shakespeare promoted his plays
15. The name of the ferris wheel ride on the River Thames

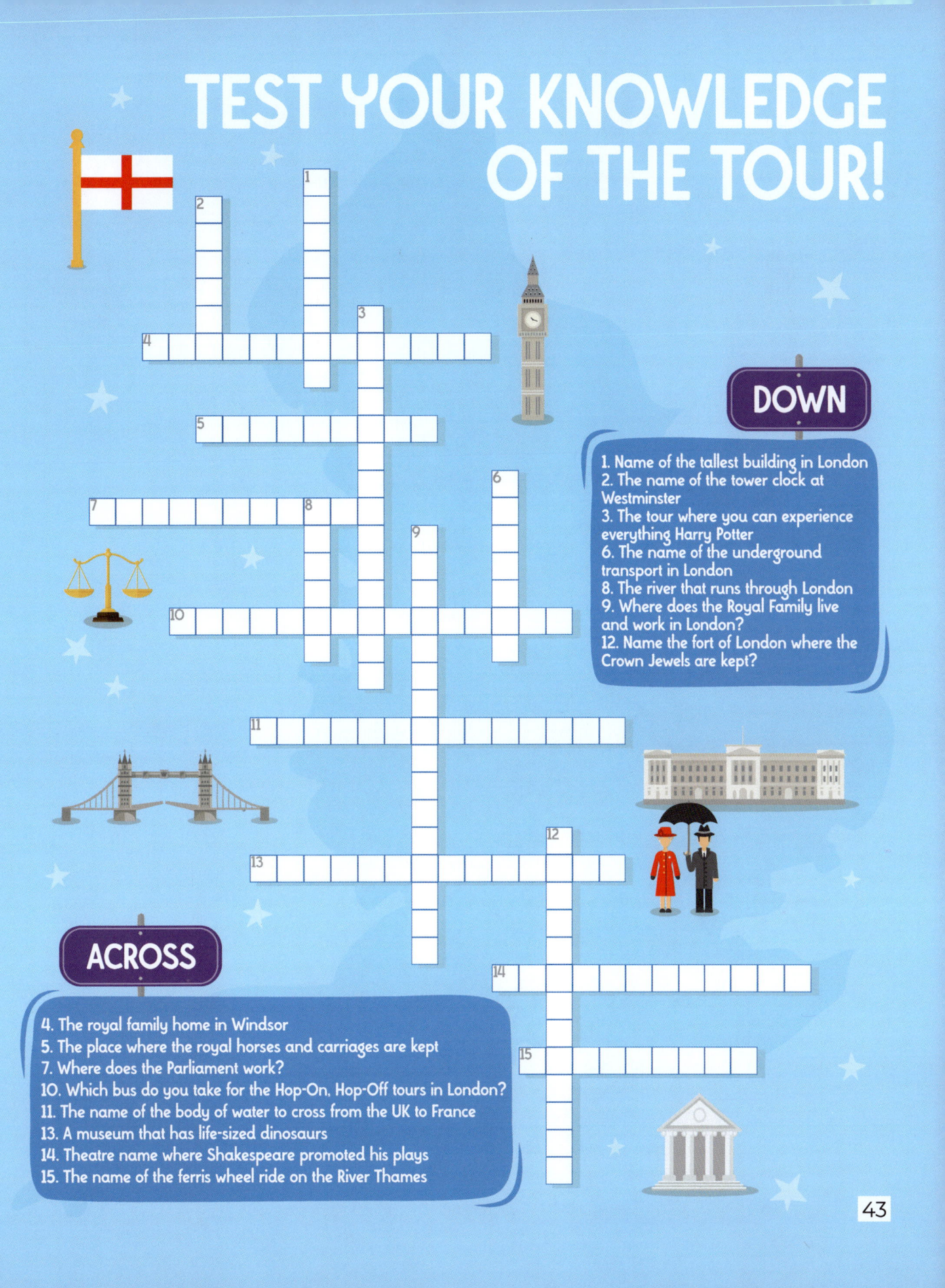

43

LONDON CULTURE!

DOWN

1. A famous book written about an ogre
2. What is the currency called in the UK?
4. A famous detective
5. Ashley's favorite tour
6. Name of taxis that are famous for the drivers memorizing the streets of London
8. The name of very large homes built throughout the UK
14. The name of the future king of England
16. A law in the UK that says you can walk on private property throughout England
17. What kind of dog did the former queen love
19. What do Brits call American Soccer?

ACROSS

3. Where the royal horses and carriages are taken care of and trained for big events
6. What do the British call themselves for short?
7. The name of the king of England
9. Name the famous artist who nobody has seen, but paints on the streets in the UK
10. A famous football player who was with Manchester United
11. Name the famous "posh" horse race where everyone dresses up and wears hats, tops and tails
12. Andrew's favorite tour
13. A famous movie with a magical nanny
15. The type of dog named Poppy that Ashley and Andrew met in Hyde Park
18. The type of dog named Merlin that was also Queen Elizabeth's favorite
20. Name the famous bear that appeared on TV recently with Queen Elizabeth
21. Name a famous movie for kids that features a boy that has wings and can fly

UK ENGLISH

```
D R E S S I N G G O W N S R
B T M S B O I R E E H C P U
F O C A S O R T E D L O C B
O O B U T M N T E L L H D B
O B S S I H N N O T I G U I
T S E R Y E S R E P E I S S
B S E S M O T S S T T L T H
A S O E O E U H C R O T B B
L P V N P U C R S L O E I I
L A H O O I Y R U E S L N S
P C O P P E R E I N O L I C
M O T O R W A Y B S C Y D U
T L U E T A M E U B P L O I
T S L I F T E E S V A S E T
```

BOBSYOURUNCLE TORCH   SUSS   BISCUIT
DRESSINGGOWN   MOTORWAY   MATE   CHEERIO
ABBEY   BONNET   CHIPS   TELLY
LIFT   BOOT   PAVEMENT SORTED
DUSTBIN   CRISPS   FOOTBALL PETROL
RUBBISH   COPPER   MATHS

45

FILL IN THE BLANKS

See if you can remember without looking back!
Test your knowledge about the United Kingdom!

1. What is the King of England's name? _____ _____.
2. Name the river running through London! The River _____.
3. When you take out the garbage, you are taking out the _____.
4. Instead of wearing a costume, you'll be wearing _____ _____.
5. What is the capital of Great Britain? _____.
6. The population of London is _____.
7. What are the four small countries that make up the United Kingdom:
    - _____
    - _____
    - _____
    - _____

8. What are the five countries that have dominion relationships with the UK?
    - _____
    - _____
    - _____
    - _____
    - _____

9. What is the name of the currency in the UK? The _____ _____.
10. Who's face will be on the currency in 2024? _____ _____.
11. Brits drive on the left side of the road, from which side of the car do they sit to drive? Left / Right
12. Name the body of water that you cross to get from the UK to France? _____.
13. The underground trains are called The _____.
14. If you are part of the Monarchy, you are in the _____ Family.
15. What are the four most popular professional sports in the UK?
    - _____
    - _____
    - _____
    - _____

16. How many cups of tea do the Brits make in a day? _____ million! BLIMEY!

THE MAZE TO WINDSOR CASTLE!

PLAN YOUR FAMILY TRIP

DAY #1 — These are my favorite places I want to visit:

FIRST DAY: I ARRIVE.

My flight arrives on this date _____ time _____.
It will take me ____ hour(s) to get to my hotel.
We will take _____ to get to our hotel.
It will take us ____ hours to get settled.
How many hours do I have left in the day to do something? _____

We are planning a trip to London!

DAY #2

	LOCATION	TRANSPORT TO THE NEXT STOP
Morning	_____	_____
Lunch	_____	_____
Afternoon	_____	_____
Dinner	_____	_____
Evening	_____	_____

TRAVEL TIPS: Don't forget to have breakfast in the morning before you set out!

DAY #3

	LOCATION	TRANSPORT TO THE NEXT STOP
Morning	_____	_____
Lunch	_____	_____
Afternoon	_____	_____
Dinner	_____	_____
Evening	_____	_____

DAY #4

	LOCATION	TRANSPORT TO THE NEXT STOP
Morning	_____	_____
Lunch	_____	_____
Afternoon	_____	_____
Dinner	_____	_____
Evening	_____	_____

DAY #5

	LOCATION	TRANSPORT TO THE NEXT STOP
Morning	_____	_____
Lunch	_____	_____
Afternoon	_____	_____
Dinner	_____	_____
Evening	_____	_____

DAY #6

	LOCATION	TRANSPORT TO THE NEXT STOP
Morning	_____	_____
Lunch	_____	_____
Afternoon	_____	_____
Dinner	_____	_____
Evening	_____	_____

DAY #7

LAST DAY

My flight departs on this date _____ time:_____.
It will take me ____ hour(s) to get from my hotel to the airport.
We will take the _____ to get to the airport.
We would have to leave at _____ to arrive at the airport 2 hours before our flight.
Do I have time to do something fun before going to the airport? _____
Where will we go if we have time? _____

Andrew & Ashley's EUROPEAN TOURS

DON'T FORGET TO DOWNLOAD THE LONDON TRAVEL JOURNAL!

Get the *London Travel Journal* here.

SCAN ME

Visit **AndrewandAshleysEuropeanTours.com** for more travel details, additional activities, updates on travel destinations, and more.

Cheerio or goodbye for now!

We've had some incredible experiences and seen so many new things in London so far. This visit is just the beginning! There is so much more to see in the UK and around Europe. We hope you take advantage of every minute in London to learn and try as many new things as you can, because, who knows? You may want to come back someday as an exchange student or on an epic trip with your mates!

So cheerio! Until next time.